Xavier Riddle and the Secret Museum: I am Alexander Hamilton

LEVEL 3

F&P TEXT LEVEL M

This book is perfect for a **Transitional Reader** who:
• can read multisyllable and compound words;
• can read words with prefixes and suffixes;
• is able to identify story elements (beginning, middle, end, plot, setting, characters, problem, solution); and
• can understand different points of view.

Here are some **activities** you can do during and after reading this book:
  • Character's Feelings: In this story, Yadina is nervous about leaving kindergarten. Reread the story to find text evidence that shows where she experiences these feelings. Would you feel the same way as Yadina? Why or why not?
  • Creative Writing: Pretend you are taking a boat to school for the first time. Write a journal entry about that day. How did you feel? Were you nervous or excited? Describe your adventure on the seas.

Remember, sharing the love of reading with a child is the best gift you can give!

*This book has been officially leveled by using the F&P Text Level Gradient™ leveling system.

PENGUIN YOUNG READERS
An Imprint of Penguin Random House LLC, New York

Published in 2020 by Penguin Young Readers, an imprint of Penguin Random House LLC, New York. Manufactured in China.

Visit us online at www.penguinrandomhouse.com.

ISBN 9780593096352 (pbk)   10 9 8 7 6 5 4 3 2 1
ISBN 9780593096420 (hc)   10 9 8 7 6 5 4 3 2 1

I am Alexander Hamilton

adapted by Nancy Parent

Yadina is about to have
an adventure. She is leaving
kindergarten.

"I wonder what first grade will be like," she says.

"We can show you," says Xavier. "Come on!"

Brad and Xavier walk Yadina down a long hallway.

"It's at the *very* end," says Brad.

"Are you sure it's this far?" Yadina asks.

Yadina sees her new classroom.

"It's so big," she says. "And different."

"Don't worry," Xavier says. "It'll be great."

Yadina does not think so. "I'm *not* going to first grade," she says.

"To the Secret Museum!" Xavier says.

"Um . . . ," Brad says.

The friends run to the Secret Museum and see an object rise from the floor.

"It's a really big coin," says Brad.

"Like pirate treasure," says Xavier.

Berby beeps two beeps.

A figure appears. "It's Alexander Hamilton," Xavier says.

"I hope he can help me stay in kindergarten," says Yadina.

"There's only one way to find out!"
says Xavier.

They all put two hands on Berby.
There's a giant burst of light.

The three friends find Alexander Hamilton near a shop. "I'm off on a big adventure," he tells them.

"Where are you going?" asks Yadina.

"I'm going to school," Alexander says.

"Just like you, Yadina!" says Xavier.

"My school is far away," says
Alexander. "Want to walk with me?"

The three friends follow
Alexander. "I'm a little nervous. But
I'm mostly excited!" he says.

"Really?" asks Yadina.

"New adventures are exciting!"

says Alexander.

Alexander pulls out a map.

His school is very far away.

"How will you get there?" says Brad.

"On that boat," says Alexander.

"Are you sure you want to go to a *new* place with *new* people?" asks Yadina.

"That's what makes it an adventure!" says Alexander.

He waves goodbye as the boat
leaves the dock.

Berby appears again. She sends
the friends to Philadelphia. They find
Alexander Hamilton.

"Welcome!" he says. "I finished school."

"Really?" says Yadina.

"And then I helped make a brand-new country: the United States," he says. "Want to see my latest adventure?"

He shows them all a coin press. "These are the very first United States coins," says Alexander.

Alexander shows one of the coins to his friend, too. It's George Washington!

"Alexander Hamilton went to school," says Yadina. "And look what happened!"

"He helped make a brand-new country," says Brad.

"And got a super cool job in charge of shiny coins!" says Xavier.

"I think it's time to have my own adventure!" says Yadina.

"Let's go home."

Now Yadina wants to go to school. "I am ready for first grade!" she says. "Because new adventures are exciting, just like Alexander Hamilton said!"